Pioneers of Light and Sound

Connie Jankowski

Physical Science Readers:
Pioneers of Light and Sound

Publishing Credits

Editorial Director
Dona Herweck Rice

Associate Editor
Joshua BishopRoby

Editor-in-Chief
Sharon Coan, M.S.Ed.

Creative Director
Lee Aucoin

Illustration Manager
Timothy J. Bradley

Publisher
Rachelle Cracchiolo, M.S.Ed.

Science Contributor
Sally Ride Science

Science Consultants
Michael E. Kopecky,
Science Department Chair,
Chino Hills High School
Jane Weir, MPhys

Teacher Created Materials
5301 Oceanus Drive
Huntington Beach, CA 92649-1030
http://www.tcmpub.com

ISBN 978-0-7439-0580-0

Printed in China
Nordica.022019.CA21900056

Table of Contents

Discovering the World of Light and Sound

The world of light and sound is rich and beautiful. All around us are layers of sights and sounds. We see and hear thousands of things each day. They give interest and joy to nearly everything we do. Can you imagine a world without light and sound? Without light, we could not see. Without sound, we would lose an important means of experiencing the world.

Not everyone has the ability to see and hear. People who are deaf or blind are still able to find their way in the world without those senses. Even when light and sound cannot be seen or heard, they still exist.

Light also serves an important purpose. Not only does it allow things to be seen, but also it gives energy to the world. Earth as we know it would not exist without the power of light.

Scientists have studied light and sound for many years. They have found that light and sound are made of waves. Sound waves are caused by the movement of **atoms**. Atoms are the tiny particles that make up everything there is in the world. Light waves are caused by the movement of electromagnetic fields. That is the same kind of energy in electricity and used in your microwave. Scientists have also found that light waves and sound waves can be managed. Several inventors have made machines that use light and sound to help people.

The scientists who have studied light and sound have led interesting lives, too. Some dedicated their lives to science. Others had many interests. Sometimes, understanding the lives of scientists helps us to understand how discoveries are made.

Catch the Waves

Light and sound both travel in waves, much like the waves of the ocean. Light waves reflect off objects and meet the eyes. That is how we know the shape, size, and color of things. Sound waves vibrate the air around them, and ears pick up the vibrations. They send signals to the brain. The brain translates the message of the sound.

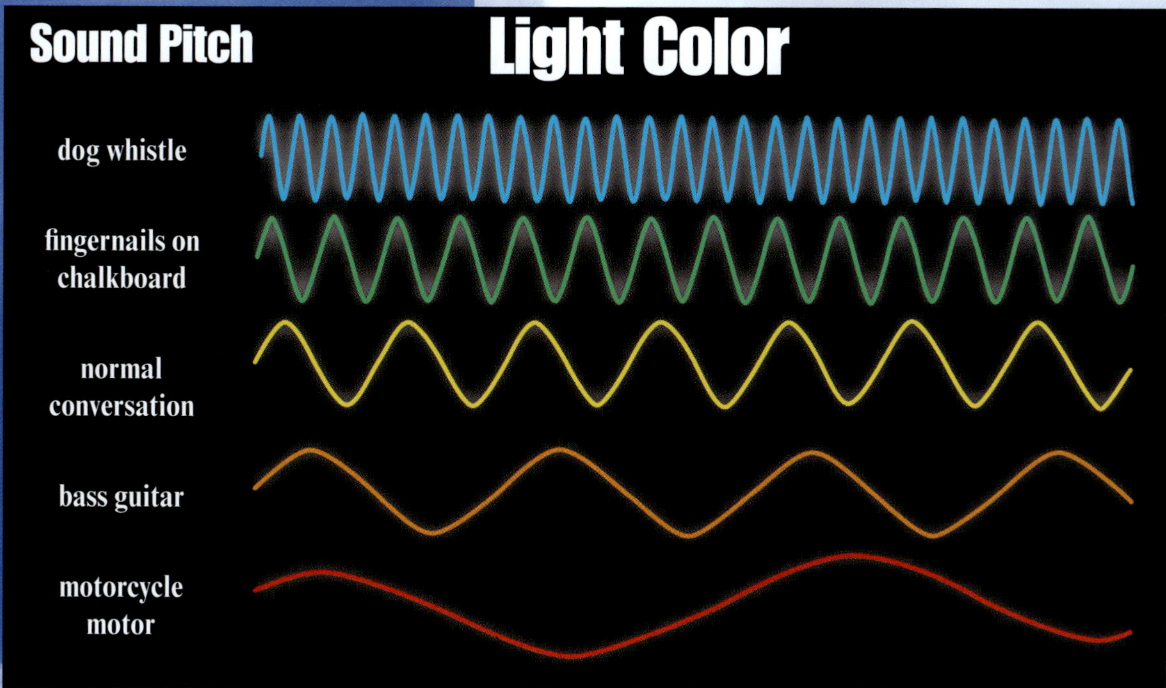

Short wavelengths that are close together make the cool colors at one end of the rainbow and high-pitched sounds. Long wavelengths that are further apart make the warm colors and low-pitched sounds at the other end of the spectrum. The top of a wave is called the peak. The bottom is the trough.

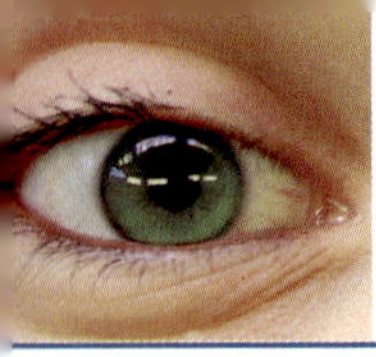

Thomas Young (1773–1829)

Thomas Young was born in England during a time of great learning in science and art. Great scientists and artists were making many new discoveries and creating new ways of expression.

Young himself was very bright from an early age. When he was two, he could read fluently. He began to learn Latin at the age of six. By the time he was 16, he knew 10 different languages. At 19, he began to study medicine. As a very bright person, he was certainly born at the right time. He fit right in with the great thinkers of his day.

As a university student, the first paper Young published was on the human eye. He believed that the muscles and structure of the eye allowed it to see. This began his path in the study of light.

While still a young man, Young's uncle died and left him a great deal of money. Young was able to follow his dreams and study what he wanted. He practiced medicine and he taught, but he didn't have to earn a living. He focused much of his time on the study of light and sound. He spent so much time and energy on them that he published many of his papers without his name. He didn't want people to think he was neglecting his other duties.

Today's Light Scientist

Dr. Kristina Johnson works with light, too. Her work is happening today. She is an expert in **optics**, which is the science of light. Her specialty is splitting light into colors. She feels strongly about educating young people. Johnson joined with a local weather person to create a television series called *Physics of Light*. It is meant to educate students about light, what it is, and what it does. She is also an inventor with more than 45 **patents**.

In Young's time, people weren't sure how light worked. Some people thought it moved in waves. Other people thought light was made of little pieces of light called corpuscles. Young performed an experiment to find out.

Young passed a beam of light through two parallel slits in a thick card. The light shone through the two slits onto the wall. If light was made of corpuscles, the light on the wall would look normal. It didn't. Instead, some parts were brighter and others were darker. This showed that light moved in waves. (This is called the **wave theory of light**.) Some of the wave peaks were combining to make the bright parts. The dark parts were where two wave troughs combined.

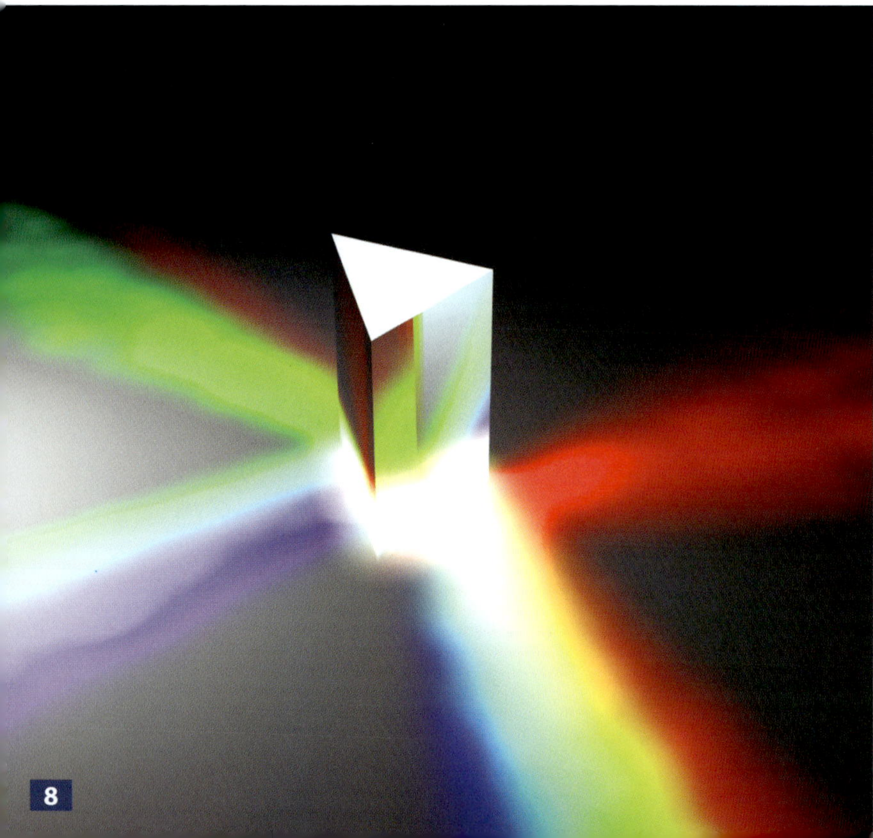

In the red end of the spectrum, there are long wavelengths, low frequency, and low amplitude. In the violet end of the spectrum, there are short wavelengths, high frequency, and high amplitude.

Later, Young also studied vision. He studied the eye and how it sees color. His discoveries led to the invention of prescription eyeglasses. Countless people who could not see well had a chance to see perfectly because of Young's experiments and the work of other scientists.

Other scientists did not immediately see the importance of Young's experiments. But a few years later, they would use his work to help advance their own. That is the way of science. One scientist's work leads to another's work. In that way, the world of science and discovery constantly grows.

Milky Way Galaxy

A Big Light

Sandra Faber is brilliant, and so is her work. Yes, she's bright, but the most brilliant thing is what she's looking at. Faber is an astronomer who studies galaxies. Galaxies are collections of stars, gas, and dust. They include about 100 billion stars each! Faber tries to learn how galaxies are made, change, and grow.

Louis-Jacques-Mandé Daguerre (1787–1851)

Louis-Jacques-Mandé Daguerre (lwee zhahk mahn-DAY duh-GAIR) was born in France. He started his career as an apprentice. An apprentice is a young person who does a job while learning from a master. His field was architecture. That is the designing of buildings. He was also a skilled artist. By the time he was 16, he became a stage designer in a Paris theater.

Daguerre's designs made him famous. He showed an amazing ability to use light and lighting effects in his designs. He also created a new type of theater that became all the rage in the 1820s. He called it **diorama**. It used changing light effects cast on giant paintings of famous places. He added real objects to the scenes. By using windows with blinds that opened and closed, he made images appear and disappear. It often looked as though an image changed from day to night. People loved to see these works of art in this way.

Louis-Jacques-Mandé Daguerre

Notice how the light in the diorama seems actually to come through the window.

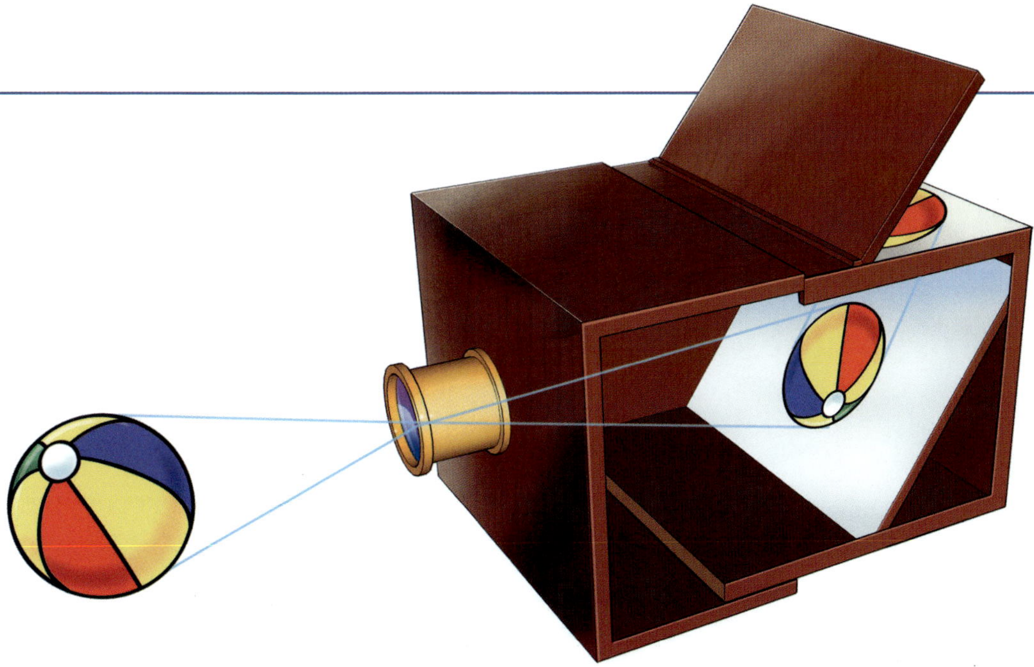

This diagram shows a camera obscura at work.

In order to make his diorama paintings, Daguerre needed something to help him capture and freeze the images. He had been using a device called a **camera obscura** to help him see images for painting. In 1835, he made a discovery with the camera obscura. In the camera obscura, he used a paper that was sensitive to light. He then left the paper in a cupboard. Days later, he noticed the paper lying there. The image he had been looking at days before through the camera obscura had appeared on the paper.

He realized that the image was there because of a broken thermometer in the cupboard. Mercury vapor from the thermometer "set" the image on the paper. In a few hours, the image disappeared again.

Michelson and Morley

The Michelson-Morley experiment is one of the most important in the history of physics and the study of light. In the late 1800s, Michelson and Morley worked together to measure the speed of light. They won the Nobel Prize for their work.

Daguerre began to experiment with this process. Finally, he was able to capture an image in just 30 minutes. Then he figured out how to make the image last. This new process was called a **daguerreotype**. It was possible because of light and chemicals combined.

The daguerreotype process is fairly simple. The process consists of the following steps.

1. Expose a copper plate to iodine. The fumes form light-sensitive silver iodide.
2. Expose the plate to light for about 20 minutes. This is where the image is made.
3. Develop the plate over heated mercury.
4. Fix the image in a salt solution.
5. Rinse the plate in hot distilled water.

The quality of the photographs was good, but there were some problems. The photos could not be reproduced. They were delicate. And the images were difficult to view from some angles.

People didn't mind any of that. From the time the discovery was announced, it was hugely popular. The era of photography began.

The process Daguerre developed is still valued today. Examples of this style have survived time and are seen in museums and private collections. Daguerre's artist eye and his scientific curiosity combined to give the world a great gift. The daguerreotype images have preserved a piece of history.

Patience, Please

People had to sit still for up to 30 minutes for a daguerreotype. Otherwise the image would be blurry. That is why people are not smiling in early photographs. They couldn't hold a smile in place that long!

Did You Know?

In the 1800s, it became popular for people to take photos of loved ones after they died. They were posed as though they were alive but asleep. These were not meant to be gruesome. People just wanted to keep memories of loved ones.

George Eastman (1854–1932)

"You press the button, we do the rest." These words were written by George Eastman. He was talking about the simple act of taking pictures.

George Eastman is known as the man who brought photography to people around the world. Before Eastman, photographers had to work very hard just to take a simple picture.

He became interested in photography on a family vacation. He began to experiment in his family's kitchen. He turned his passion into a life's work.

Eastman invented roll film and changed the way cameras worked. With that, even the common person could take a good picture. Eastman founded the Eastman Kodak Company. He registered the trademark name Kodak on September 4, 1888. Many people are surprised to learn that Eastman came up with the name Kodak by arranging some of his favorite letters into a word.

Did You Know?

Kodak products support work on NASA's Space Telescope. The telescope is designed to take images from outer space and send them to Earth for review.

Early camera

Faster Than the Speed of Light

Most people today know the work of such inventors as Daguerre and Eastman. Almost everyone has taken and enjoyed a photo. Other scientists are doing work that, while not widely known, may have even greater effects in changing the world as we know it. One of these scientists is Dr. Lene Hau. Hau has traveled faster than the speed of light! How did she do it? She didn't go faster. She made light go slower.

Light travels at 300 million meters (186,000 miles) per second. That is, when nothing is in its way. In a substance, it slows down. For example, it slows to 225 million meters (140,000 miles) per second in water. In 1999, Hau froze atoms to an extremely cold state. Light passing through them slowed a great deal to 60 kilometers (37 miles) per hour. She found she could ride a bicycle faster than light! Then, further experiments led her and her team to stop light for a split second altogether! They actually made a pulse of light start and stop and start again. There's no telling what this may mean for future discoveries.

Thomas Edison (1847–1931)

Sound travels in waves, just like light does. The study of sound has led to many great inventions. Some have helped people communicate better, such as hearing aids and **telephones**. Some bring enjoyment, such as recorded music and movies. Some inventions improve our safety, and some are used to improve our health.

Edison's electric bulb

Thomas Edison in his workshop

The advancements in use of light and sound have taken off in the last 100 years. Early pioneers of physics could hardly imagine our world today. Some scientists explored the subject of light and others studied sound. Some studied both. A very important pioneer in both light and sound is Thomas Edison.

As a young boy, Edison loved to study new things. He liked to read, too. But he didn't begin to speak until he was four years old. He did not do well in school. His teachers thought he wasn't very smart. His mother took him out of school and helped him learn at home.

When Edison was a teen, he left home and traveled around the country. He began to work as a telegraph operator. The telegraph uses electric signals sent through wires to send messages. Edison thought he could use electricity in many other ways as well.

In 1879, he made the first long-lasting light bulb. He also made a generator to bring electricity to homes and businesses so they could enjoy the light bulb and other inventions.

Hey! Is Anybody Out There?

Ann Devereaux is a communications engineer. She works for NASA. She has helped to develop communications systems on spacecraft. She was also part of the team that worked on communications for the *Mars Observer*. Who knows who Devereaux might be able to talk with in the future?

Thomas Edison's work with light changed the world. But his work with sound was also revolutionary. Among other things, he invented the **phonograph**. This invention came about after Edison worked on the telegraph and the telephone. He used what he learned about sound and worked on ways to store sounds.

Edison tested his first recording machine by reciting the nursery rhyme "Mary Had a Little Lamb" into the mouthpiece. Imagine his excitement when he heard his words played back!

Edison went on to create the first silent movie. Then, in 1904, he introduced the first "talking picture." It was called *The Great Train Robbery*. It blended moving pictures with sound.

By the time Edison died, he held over 1,000 patents for his inventions, many of which involved light and sound.

▲ Thomas Edison speaking into his phonograph

Laser Light

Simply put, lasers are devices that create beams of light. Today they are used for many things, including surgery. Dr. Elsa Garmire is an expert with lasers. She has nine patents for inventions using them. She was the first person to create a laser light show for people to come and see called "Laserium." She says only one of her patents has earned money. It uses lasers to remove graffiti from public places.

Oberlin Smith (1840–1926)

Sound and picture recording, computer hard drives, and garage door openers all came from the ideas of Oberlin Smith. He held more than 70 patents during his lifetime.

Smith had a curious mind. He liked to tinker with objects that he thought he could improve. He would work on one thing and move on to the next. If he didn't think he had time to develop something, he gave it to others. That is exactly what happened with his sound-recording device.

Edison's phonograph inspired Smith. He spent many months making a recording system. Finally, he invented magnetic recording. This used the power of magnetism to record sound. He didn't patent the device, though. He didn't think he had time to tinker with it any more. So, he published his plans in a magazine. That meant he gave it to anyone in the world who wanted to use it, improve it, and make money from it.

Smith's ideas about recording inspired other scientists. One scientist used Smith's work to invent the **telegraphone**. It used a telephone, **electromagnet**, and wire to create a recording device. It was used as a telephone answering machine and voice recorder. Modern tape recorders, answering machines, and computers use the same technology.

Doppler Effect

Ever notice how a sound that gets nearer to you becomes higher in pitch? **Pitch** is how high or low a sound is. Think of a train that approaches while you're standing nearby. Its bells, whistles, and roar become higher the nearer it draws. They become lower again as it moves away. This is called the **Doppler effect**.

Sound is made through the vibration of waves. The waves have a frequency. The frequency of a sound determines its pitch. High-pitched sound has a higher frequency. Low-pitch sounds have a lower frequency.

As the train nears you, the sound waves ahead of it get pushed closer together. The sound is pitched higher. Then when the train passes you, the sound waves behind it get stretched out. The sound is pitched lower.

Alexander Graham Bell (1847–1922)

Can you imagine life without telephones? How often each day do you make a call? Many people use the phone many times a day. It keeps people in touch. Businesses depend on phones. They need phone systems for FAX machines, computers, and pagers. Telephones keep the world running.

Alexander Graham Bell filed the first patent for the telephone. Many other people invented similar machines about the same time. Bell's design beat all the others. He made his fortune from the invention.

Bell's mother was deaf. His father was a speech teacher for people who could not hear. Bell was his assistant. He fell in love with a deaf woman, Mabel Hubbard, and married her. Bell's inventions began when he tried to find ways to help teach speech to the deaf.

Bell speaking into an early model telephone

Bell became interested in electricity and what it could do for the deaf. He thought that electricity could be used to create sound or to allow the deaf to hear. He experimented with ways to send voice sounds with electricity.

In 1876, he succeeded. Using the first telephone, he sent this famous message to his assistant. "Mr. Watson, come here. I want to see you."

Metal Detectors

Bell also invented the metal detector. In 1881, President Garfield was shot. Bell gave investigators a metal detector to look for the bullet in the president's body. They forgot that Garfield's hospital bed had metal springs. The metal detector did not forget. It reacted to every inch of his body!

Today, metal detectors are used for serious business and for fun, too. Soldiers use them to look for bombs. In airports, everyone must pass through a metal detector before boarding a plane. Some people just have fun using a metal detector to find "buried treasure."

Bell patented his invention. Others claimed the telephone was their idea. Finally, the U.S. Supreme Court agreed with Bell. He won the patent. He started the Bell Telephone Company. Slowly, phones became common in houses and businesses everywhere. Today, phones can be found in almost every part of the world.

In his life, Bell held 30 patents. He kept trying to find good ways to teach the deaf to speak. He improved Edison's invention of the phonograph. Other people used or improved many of Bell's ideas, too. For example, his basic ideas were used to invent the tape recorder.

Bell speaking into his telephone

Acoustics Expert

Acoustics is the branch of science that studies sound. Acoustical engineering is the science of making buildings so that sound carries well within them. Victoria Cerami is an expert in acoustical engineering. She first learned about acoustics from her father. He was also an engineer and acoustics expert with an acoustics business. When he died, Cerami took over his business. She was just 27 years old. She was also a woman in a business that is mainly run by men. She rose to the challenge.

Today, Cerami's company makes millions of dollars a year. She does acoustic work in businesses around the world, from IMAX theaters to courthouses. She says that courtrooms are especially tough for making the right acoustics. Judges and lawyers must be sure that when they need to speak privately, others cannot hear them. Cerami must figure out how to do that.

Cerami is impressive for one more big reason. She is a two-time cancer survivor. Part of her work as a scientist is dedicated to cancer research and education.

Chemical Engineer: Jan Talbot

University of California, San Diego

Being Positive Pays Off

In college, Jan Talbot's hardest subject was chemistry. She decided to make it her focus. That's right. She decided that would give her a good challenge.

In her chemistry classes there were hundreds of students. Sometimes she was the only woman. When the professor would say, "Good morning, gentlemen," she would wave her hand to remind him she was there, too!

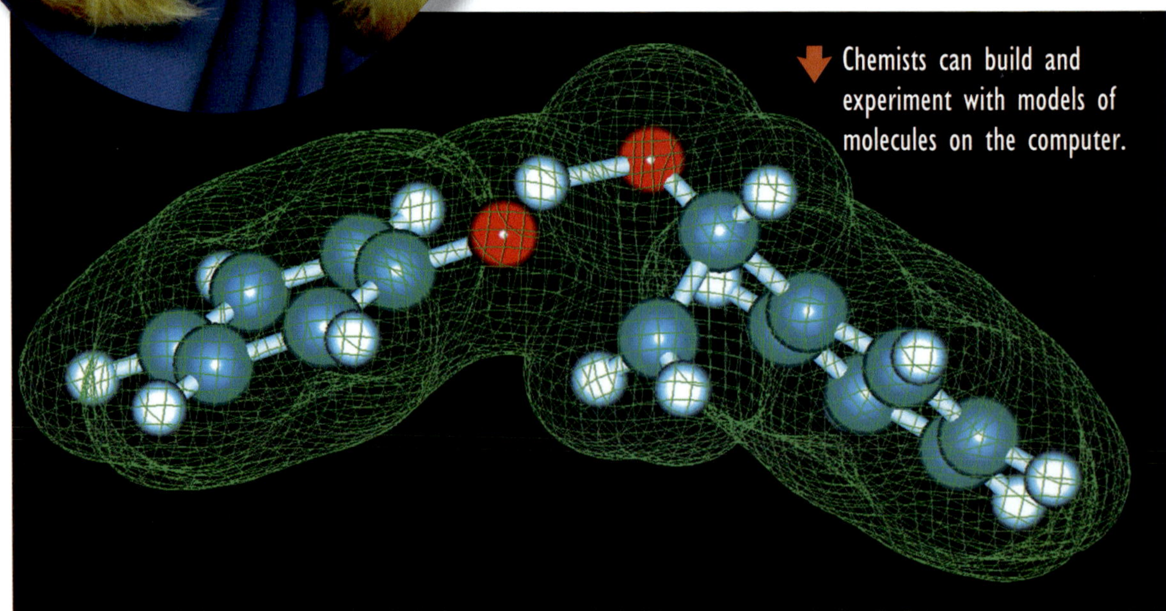

Chemists can build and experiment with models of molecules on the computer.

Talbot says she never got discouraged. "When you care about something, you don't listen to people who say you can't," she says. Being positive has paid off. Today, Talbot is a very successful chemical engineer. She uses chemistry to make things such as flat-panel screens for computers and televisions.

Experts Tell Us . . .

Why is Talbot a chemical engineer instead of a chemist? A chemist might study the reaction between two chemicals. A chemical engineer would figure out if the reaction solves any problems in the real world. "I like chemistry, but I really want to know how to use it to make something."

Think About It

Have people ever told you that you couldn't do something? What did you do about it?

Talbot enjoys a challenge such as a hike in the desert.

Lab: *Make a Periscope*

Periscopes have been used for many years. Submarine sailors use them to see above water. Doctors use a type of periscope to look inside the body. Using the principles of light from this book, you can make your own periscope.

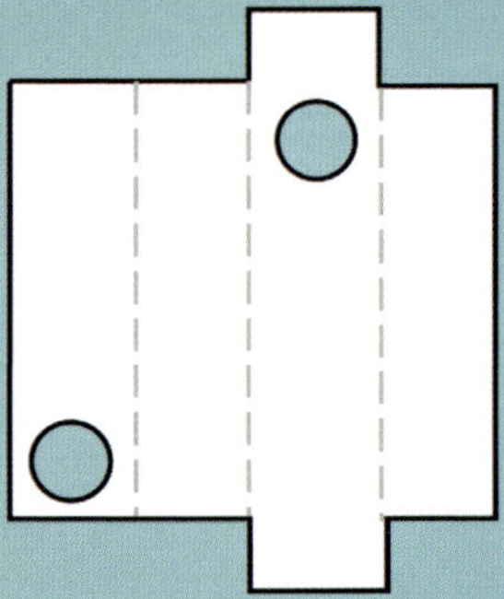

Materials

- 2 small mirrors
- stiff cardboard
- craft knife (only used with adult help)
- glue (strong enough to support a mirror)
- masking tape or wide clear tape

Procedure

1 Build the body of your periscope from cardboard. Follow the pattern shown on this page to create a hollow shaft to support your mirrors. Note the position of the tabs. Trace and cut the pattern from the cardboard. Take care when cutting the round holes.

2. Fold the cardboard along the dotted lines on the pattern. It may help to score the folds with a craft knife to make the bending easier.

3. Assemble the shaft (box). Fold the sides as shown. Tape the long side closed to form a rectangular tube with flaps. Leave the top and bottom flaps open. Lay the box on its back with the top hole on your right side.

4. Attach a strip of tape to the edge of a mirror. Slide the mirror into the box end with the reflecting side up. (You should be looking into the mirror when you look into the hole.) Tape or glue the mirror in place.

5. Turn the box end up, with the mirror at the top. Push the mirror to angle it at 45 degrees. Be sure you can close the box lid over the mirror. Support the angle by taping reinforcements to hold the mirror in place.

6. Turn the box and repeat the procedure to install the second mirror.

7. Enjoy your periscope! Keep a notebook of the things you can observe.

Glossary

acoustic—relating to sound, hearing, or the science of sound

amplitude—the extent or range of a quality, property, or process

atom—the smallest particle of an element

camera obscura—a darkened chamber in which the real image of an object is received through a small opening or lens and focused in natural color onto a facing surface rather than recorded on a film or plate

diorama—a three-dimensional miniature scene in which figures and objects are arranged in a setting against a painted background

daguerreotype—the first successfully produced type of photograph

Doppler effect—an apparent shift in the frequency of sound or light due to relative motion between the source of the sound or light and the observer

frequency—the number of times per second that crests of waves pass a checkpoint

optics—relating to the eye or vision

patent—a grant made by a government agency that gives the creator of an invention the sole right to make, use, and sell that invention for a set period of time

phonograph—the first device for recording and replaying sound

physics—the science of matter and energy and of interactions between the two

pitch—the property of a sound determined by the frequency of the waves producing it

telegraphone—an instrument for recording sound

telephone—a device that uses a system of wires, along which electrical signals are sent, through which sounds such as the human voice can be transmitted

wave theory of light—the theory that light is transmitted as waves

wavelength—the distance along a straight line from one peak of the wave to the next

Index

Sally Ride Science

Sally Ride Science™ is an innovative content company dedicated to fueling young people's interests in science. Our publications and programs provide opportunities for students and teachers to explore the captivating world of science—from astrobiology to zoology. We bring science to life and show young people that science is creative, collaborative, fascinating, and fun.

Image Credits

Cover (back) Patrick Hermans/Shutterstock; cover (front) Library of Congress; p.3 Bella D/Shutterstock; p.4 (top) Photos.com; p.5 (back) Photos.com; p.5 (front) Tim Bradley; p.6 (top) Andres Rodriguez/Shutterstock; p.6 (bottom) The Granger Collection, New York; p.7 (left) Photos.com; p.7 (right) Courtesy of Duke University; p.8 (top) Lexy Sinnott/Shutterstock; p.8 (bottom) Lexy Sinnott/Shutterstock; p.9 (top) Jeff Davies/Shutterstock; p.9 (front) AIP Emilio Segre Visual Archives; p.10 (top) Library of Congress; p.10 (left) Library of Congress; p.10 (right) Michael Freeman/Corbis; p.11 Tim Bradley; p.12 Library of Congress; p.13 Library of Congress; p.14 (top) Library of Congress; p.14 (left) Library of Congress; p.14 (right) Richard Sargeant/Shutterstock; p.15 Rick Reason; p.15 (bottom) Photos.com; p.16 (top) Menna/Shutterstock; p.16 (left) Library of Congress; p.16-17 The Granger Collection, New York; p.17 NASA; p.18 Library of Congress; p.19 (back) Steve Shoup/Shutterstock; p.19 (front) Rick Reason; p.20 (top) Library of Congress; p.20 (bottom) Rick Reason; p.21 Wessel du Plooy/Shutterstock; p.22 (top) Library of Congress; p.22 (bottom) Bettmann/Corbis; p.23 Anna Dzondzua/Shutterstock; p.24 Library of Congress; p.25 (back) Photos.com; p.25 (front) Rick Reason; p.26 (top) Jan Talbot; p.26 (bottom) Oakridge National Laboratory; p.27 Jan Talbot; p.28 (top) Clipart; p.28-29 Nicoll Rager Fuller; p.32 Getty Images